Gallery Books
Editor: Peter Fallon

BREAKING NEWS

Ciaran Carson

BREAKING NEWS

Gallery Books

Breaking News
is first published
simultaneously in paperback
and in a clothbound edition
on 27 March 2003.

The Gallery Press
Loughcrew
Oldcastle
County Meath
Ireland

ISBN 1 85235 339 2 (*paperback*)
    1 85235 340 6 (*clothbound*)

A CIP catalogue record for this book
is available from the British Library.

The Gallery Press acknowledges the financial assistance
of An Chomhairle Ealaíon / The Arts Council, Ireland.

Contents

in memoriam
William Howard Russell
1820-1907

Belfast

east

beyond the yellow
shipyard cranes

a blackbird whistles
in a whin bush

west

beside the motorway
a black taxi

rusts in a field
of blue thistles

Home

hurtling from
the airport down
the mountain road

past barbed wire
snagged with
plastic bags

fields of scrap
and thistle
farmyards

from the edge
of the plateau
my eye zooms

into the clarity
of Belfast
streets

shipyards
domes
theatres

British Army
helicopter
poised

motionless
at last

I see everything

The Gladstone Bar *circa* 1954

two men are
unloading beer

you can smell
the hops and yeast

the smouldering
heap of dung

just dropped by
one

of the great
blinkered drayhorses

Trap

backpack radio
antenna

twitching
rifle

headphones
cocked

I don't
read you

what the

over

Breaking

red alert
car parked

in a red
zone

about to

disintegrate
it's

oh

so quiet

you can
almost

hear it rust

News

alarms
shrill

lights
flash

as dust
clears

above
the paper

shop

The Belfast Telegraph
sign reads

     fast   *rap*

Horse at Balaklava, 1854

one minute

muscles rippling
glossy flank

flowing mane
the picture of life

the next

ripped open by
a shell

from chest
to loin

as by a
surgeon's knife

remark

the glaring eyeball
and distended nostril

gnashed teeth

next year rotting
harness

a debris of skin
and leather

straps
cloth and buckles

collapsed about
the skeleton

Russia

after Isaac Babel

the knife
glitters

as she slits
fish

guts slithering
into a

zinc bucket

more drink
the soldiers cry

warts blaze
on the faces

of the serving-men

Shop Fronts

cheek by jowl

chemist
tobacconist

Wilkinson Sword
razor-blades

Warhorse
plug

Wire

I met him
in a bar

he shook

my hand

spoke
of coffee-grinders

this

and that

time
and place

by now

he'd lit

a cigarette

he reeked of
explosive

Breath

watching
helicopter

gone

there's a
clear blue

space

above
my head

I feel

rinsed

clean

you know
that quiet

when the
washing-machine

stops
shuddering

Blink

everyone is
watching everybody

in the grey light
of surveillance

people hurtle
through shop

windows or are
sucked back

at a touch of the
rewind button

everyone eyes
everyone

down to the cut
and colour

of their clothes
the pattern

of the retina
the fingerprint

the bits
and pieces

being matched
as everyone

identifies
with this or that

their whereabouts
being watched

War

Sergeant Talbot
had his head

swept off
by a

round-shot

yet for half
a furlong

more

the body kept
the saddle

horse and rider
charging on

regardless

The Indian Mutiny

There I was
looking down the muzzle
of a hostile gun

with a spyglass —
I think, said I, they're
going to fire at us,

and as I spoke, *pluff*
came a spurt of smoke
with a red tongue in it —

a second of
suspense, when *whi-s-s-h*, right
for us came the round-shot

within a foot
of our heads, and plumped
into the ground a storm

of dust and grit
with which we upped and away
and into the courtyard.

No one asked us
for our passes
as we climbed the staircase

to the upper room through
heaps of glass and broken mirrors,
tapestries and beds of silk,

to stare into the blue beyond
of palaces and azure minarets,
domes, temples, colonnades

and long façades
of fair perspective. Look for miles
away, and still

the ocean spreads,
the towers of the city
gleam amidst it,

spires of gold
and constellated spheres
so bright

I had to rub my eyes
before this vision
vaster and more beautiful

than Paris; down
another staircase then,
into a courtyard

large as Temple Gardens
bounded by a range of palaces
of gilt and stucco:

green shutters
and Venetian blinds occlude
the apertures which pierce

the walls in double rows,
and there are statues, fountains,
orange-groves, aqueducts

and kiosks, burnished domes
of metal, fresco paintings
on the blind-windows.

Through all these
the soldiery run riot,
forcing their way

into the long corridors —
you hear the crack
of musketry, the crash

of glass, as little jets
of smoke curl out from
the closed lattices.

The orange-groves
are strewn with dead
and dying sepoys,

the white statues
drenched with red.
Against a smiling Venus

a British soldier shot
through the neck
pumps gouts of blood

and soldiers drunk
with plunder pour out
from the broken portals

bearing china vases,
teapots, lamp-shades, mirrors,
which they dash to pieces,

others busy gouging
the precious stones
from stems of pipes,

from saddle-cloths, from
hilts of swords, from pistol-butts,
their bodies swathed

in gem-encrusted stuffs:
court after court
connected by arched passageways

where lie the dead sepoys,
clothes smouldering
on their flesh.

One who had his brains
dashed out by round-shot
made me think —

minutes telescoped
into each other — twelve inches
lower and I'd not

be here to write
nor would you read
this news of how

we freed Lucknow.

Some Uses of a Dead Horse

the bones give
buttons

snuff-boxes
and knife-handles

the hooves
yield

a beautiful
Prussian blue

the shoes
shot

Detail

men and horses
fell

in swathes
like grass before

a scythe
but I was saved

by this

he opened
the Bible

to reveal
the bullet

stopped
at Revelation

Waste Not

birds flock
above the field

near
dark

women with shears
attend

the dead
harvesting

gold braid
and buttons

In St Patrick's Cathedral, Dublin

British Army
regimental

colours
flown

in this
campaign

or that

now

hang

tattered by
the moth

or shot

Skip

I'm writing
this

in a black flip-
top police

notebook
I gleaned

from the
bomb-

damage
of Her Majesty's

Stationery Office

Fragment

from a piece of
the Tupperware
lunchbox that held

the wiring

they could tell
the bombmaker wore
Marigold rubber gloves

Campaign

shot
the horse fell

a crow
plucked the eyes

time passed

from a socket
crept

a butterfly

Spin Cycle

here it comes
again I said

I couldn't
hear

myself
speak for the

thug-thug

helicopter
overhead

I put in
the ear-plugs

everything went
centrifugal

Spin Cycle 2

gun-gun

ear-plugs in

blank-blank

Harvest

a swathe
of honeyed light

cuts through
the gunsmoke

swarms
of men and horses

crawl
all over

the wheat
and barley fields

like mutilated
bees

Théodore Géricault: *Farrier's Signboard*, 1814

he holds
the reins

of the massive
straining draught

horse in one
fist hammer

in the other
man and horse

deadlocked
raked by light

before the red
glow of the forge

this

painted in oil
directly on to

roughly carpentered
gap-jointed

boards
a door

or shutter
wood

and nail heads
showing through

this the year
before Waterloo

The Forgotten City

after William Carlos Williams, 'The Forgotten City'

When on a day of the last disturbances
I was returning from the country, trees
were across the road, thoroughfares and side streets
barricaded: burning trucks and buses, walls
of ripped-up paving-stones, sheets of corrugated
iron fencing, storm-gratings, brown torrents
gushing from a broken water main.
I had to take what road I could to find
my way back to the city. My bike hissed
over crisp wet tarmac as I cycled through
extraordinary places: long deserted avenues
and driveways leading to apartment blocks,
car-ports, neo-Tudor churches, cenotaphs,
and in one place an acre or more of
rusting Nissen huts left over from the War. Parks.
It was so quiet that at one gatekeeper's lodge
I could hear coffee perking. I passed
a crematorium called Roselawn, pleasant
cul-de-sacs and roundabouts with names
I never knew existed. Knots of men and women
gathered here and there at intersections
wearing hats and overcoats, talking
to themselves, gesticulating quietly.
I had no idea where I was and promised myself
I would go back some day and study this
grave people. How did they achieve
such equilibrium? How did they get
cut off in this way from the stream of
bulletins, so under-represented

in our parliaments and media when so near
the troubled zone, so closely surrounded
and almost touched by the famous and familiar?

Minus

no
helicopter

noise
this hour

gone by
the room

still
dark

I raise
the blind

on
a moon

so bright
it hurts

and oh
so cold

my breath
sounds

like frost

Francisco Goya: *The Third of May 1808*, 1814

behold
the man

who faces
the stream

of light
white-shirted

arms
flung

open
to receive

the volley
offering

the firing-squad
his ghost

he is not
blindfolded

Last Effect

take
the watch

feel
the weight

of its bullet-
dented case

the Braille

of its
glassless dial

hands
arrested

at the minute
and the hour

of his salvation
death

postponed
for years

until that
yesterday

he failed
to see

O what is time
my friend

when faced with
eternity

Siege

the road
to Sevastopol

is paved
with round-shot

the road
from Sevastopol

with boots
that lack feet

Exile

night
after night

I walk

the smouldering
dark streets

Sevastopol
Crimea

Inkerman
Odessa

Balkan
Lucknow

Belfast
is many

places then
as now

all lie
in ruins

and
it is

as much
as I can do

to save
even one

from oblivion

Wake

near dawn

boom

the window
trembled

bomb

I thought

then in
the lull

a blackbird
whistled in

a chink
of light

between
that world

and this

Edward Hopper: *Early Sunday Morning,* 1939

clear
blue sky above

upper storey
blinds half-drawn

not a soul about
the strip

of shop fronts
only a red

white and blue
barber's pole

and a fire
hydrant

casting
shadows

on the sidewalk
from the east

beyond
the frame

immeasurably
long

another shadow
falls

from what
we cannot see

to what
we cannot see

dawn
before the War

The War Correspondent

1

Gallipoli

Take sheds and stalls from Billingsgate,
glittering with scaling-knives and fish,
the tumbledown outhouses of English farmers' yards
that reek of dung and straw, and horses
cantering the mewsy lanes of Dublin;

take an Irish landlord's ruinous estate,
elaborate pagodas from a Chinese Delftware dish
where fishes fly through shrouds and sails and yards
of leaking ballast-laden junks bound for Benares
in search of bucket-loads of tea as black as tin;

take a dirty gutter from a back street in Boulogne,
where shops and houses teeter so their pitched roofs meet,
some chimney stacks as tall as those in Sheffield
or Irish round towers,
smoking like a fleet of British ironclad destroyers;

take the garlic-oregano-tainted arcades of Bologna,
linguini-twists of souks and smells of rotten meat,
as labyrinthine as the rifle-factories of Springfield,
or the tenements deployed by bad employers
who sit in parlours doing business drinking *Power's*;

then populate this slum with Cypriot and Turk,
Armenians and Arabs, British riflemen
and French Zouaves, camel-drivers, officers, and sailors,
sappers, miners, Nubian slaves, Greek money-changers,
plus interpreters who do not know the lingo;

dress them in turbans, shawls of fancy needlework,
fedoras, fezzes, sashes, shirts of fine Valenciennes,
boleros, pantaloons designed by jobbing tailors,
knickerbockers of the ostrich and the pink flamingo,
sans-culottes, and outfits even stranger;

requisition slaughter-houses for the troops,
and stalls with sherbet, lemonade, and rancid lard for sale,
a temporary hospital or two, a jail,
a stagnant harbour redolent with cholera,
and open sewers running down the streets;

let the staple diet be green cantaloupes
swarming with flies washed down with sour wine,
accompanied by the Byzantine
jangly music of the cithara
and the multi-lingual squawks of parakeets —

O landscape riddled with the diamond mines of Kimberley,
and all the oubliettes of Trebizond,
where opium-smokers doze among the Persian rugs,
and spies and whores in dim-lit snugs
discuss the failing prowess of the Allied powers,

where prowling dogs sniff for offal beyond
the stench of pulped plums and apricots,
from which is distilled the brandy they call 'grape-shot',
and soldiers lie dead or drunk among the crushed flowers —
I have not even begun to describe Gallipoli.

2

Varna

On the night of August 10th, a great fire broke out,
destroying utterly a quarter of the town.
A stiff breeze fanned the flames along the tumbledown
wooden streets. Things were not helped by the current drought.

It began in the spirit store of the French commissariat.
The officers in charge immediately broached the main vat,
but, as the liquid spouted down the streets, a Greek
was seen to set fire to it in a fit of drunken pique.

He was cut down to the chin by a French lieutenant,
and fell into the blazing torrent. The howls of the inhabitants,
the clamour of women, horses, children, dogs, the yells
of prisoners trapped in their cells,

were appalling. Marshal St Arnaud displayed great coolness
in supervising the operations of the troops;
but both the French and we were dispossessed
of immense quantities of goods —

barrels of biscuit, nails, butter, and bullets,
carpenters' tool-boxes, hat-boxes, cages of live pullets,
polo-sticks, Lord Raglan's portable library of books,
and 19,000 pairs of soldiers' boots.

A consignment of cavalry sabres was found
amid the ruins, fused into the most fantastic shapes,
looking like an opium-smoker's cityscape
or a crazy oriental fairground —

minarets, cathedral spires of twisted blades, blades
wrought into galleries and elevated switchbacks,
railroad sidings, cul-de-sacs, trolleyways, and racing tracks,
gazebos, pergolas, trellises, and colonnades.

Such were the effects of the great fire of Varna.
Next day the cholera broke out in the British fleets
anchored in the bay, then spread into the streets,
and for weeks thousands of souls sailed into Nirvana.

3

Dvno

Once I gazed on these meadows
incandescent with poppies,
buttercups and cornflowers
surrounded by verdant hills

in which lay deep shady dells,
dripping ferns shower-dappled
under the green canopy
of live oaks and wild apples,

aspens, weeping-willow, ash,
maple, plane, rhododendron,
sweet chestnut, spruce, Douglas fir,
and Cedar of Lebanon,

round which vines and acacias
vied with wild clematises
to climb ever on and up
to twine the trunks of the trees,

and I thought I was in Eden,
happily stumbling about
in a green Irish garden
knee-deep in potato flowers.

But at night a fog descends,
as these woods breed miasmas,
and slithering through the brush
are snakes thick as a man's arm;

the vapours rise and fatten
on the damp air, becoming
palpable as mummy shrouds,
creeping up from the valleys

fold after fold in the dark,
to steal into a man's tent,
and wrap him, as he's sleeping,
in their deadly cerements.

One day, down by the sea-shore,
I scraped my name with a stick
on the sand, and discovered
the rotting face of a corpse;

and by night in the harbour
phosphorescent bodies float
up from the murky bottom
to drift moonward past the fleet

like old wooden figureheads,
bobbing torsos bolt upright.
Tiger, Wasp, Bellerophon,
Niger, Arrow, Terrible,

Vulture, Viper, Albion,
Britannia, Trafalgar,
Spitfire, Triton, Oberon:
these are vessels I remember.

As for the choleraic dead,
their names have been unravelled
like their bones, whose whereabouts
remain unknown.

4

Balaklava

The Turks marched in dense columns, bristling with steel.
Sunlight flashed on the polished barrels of their firelocks
and on their bayonets, relieving their sombre hue,
for their dark blue uniforms looked quite black
when viewed *en masse*. The Chasseurs d'Afrique,
in light powder-blue jackets, with white cartouche belts, scarlet
pantaloons, mounted on white Arabs, caught the eye
like a bed of flowers scattered over the valley floor.

Some, indeed, wore poppies red as cochineal,
plucked from the rich soil, which bore an abundance of
    hollyhocks,
dahlias, anemones, wild parsley, mint, whitethorn, rue,
sage, thyme, and countless other plants whose names I lack.
As the Turkish infantry advanced, their boots creaked
and crushed the springy flowers, and delicate
perfumes wafted into the air beneath the April sky:
the smell of sweating men and horses smothered by flora.

Waving high above the more natural green
of the meadow were phalanxes of rank grass, marking the
    mounds
where the slain of October 25th had found their last repose,
and the snorting horses refused to eat those deadly shoots.
As the force moved on, more evidences of that fatal day
came to light. The skeleton of an English horseman
had tatters of scarlet cloth hanging to the bones of his arms;
all the buttons had been cut off the jacket.

Round as shot, the bullet-skull had been picked clean
save for two swatches of red hair. The remains of a wolfhound
sprawled at his feet. From many graves, the uncovered bones
of the tenants had started up, all of them lacking boots.
Tangled with rotted trappings, half-decayed horses lay
where they'd fallen. Fifes and drums struck up a rataplan;
so we swept on over our fellow men-at-arms
under the noon sun in our buttoned-up jackets.

5

Kertch

A row of half a mile
across the tideless sea
brought us to a beautiful beach

edged by a green sward
dotted with whitewashed houses
through which the French

were running riot, swords
in hand, breaking in windows
and doors, pursuing hens:

every house we entered
ransacked, every cupboard
with a pair of red breeches

sticking out of it, and a blue
coat inside of it; barrels of lard,
bags of sour bread, mattress feathers,

old boots, statues, icons, strewn
on the floors, the furniture
broken to kindling —

such an awful stench
from the broken jars of fish oil
and the rancid butter,

the hens and ducks cackling,
bundled by the feet
by Zouaves and Chasseurs,

who, fancied up in old calico
dresses, pranced about
the gardens like princesses.

I was reminded of Palmyra
after we had sacked it:
along the quay a long line

of walls, which once
were the fronts of storehouses,
magazines, mansions, and palaces —

now empty shells,
hollow and roofless, lit from within
by lurid fires,

as clouds of incense
rose from the battered domes
and ruined spires,

all deadly silent
save for the infernal noise
of soldiers playing on pianos

with their boot-heels,
and the flames crackling
within the walls

Then they'd return, regular as clockwork,
after feeding behind the Russian lines.
I know, for I remember my watch stopped,
and we made a sundial with white stones.

The Tchernaya abounded with wildfowl.
Some of the officers had little hides
of their own where they went at night to kill
time. This was deemed highly exciting sport,

for the Russian batteries at Inkerman,
if their sentries were properly alert,
would send two or three shells at the sportsmen,
who took short odds on escaping unhurt.

In the daytime, they'd take two or three French
soldiers down with them to act as decoys,
who were only too glad of the break. Hence
we coined the old saying, 'dead as a duck'.

Then there was betting on how many flies
would fill a jar in which lay a dead dove,
and the two-or-three-legged dog races —
little to do? There was never enough.

Thus we spent the time by the Tchernaya,
making it up as we went along, till
long before the battle of Tchernaya,
we each had two or three life-stories to tell.

7

Sedan

Cavalry men asleep
on their horses' necks.
In the fields, heaps

of sodden troops,
the countryside charming,
covered with rich crops,

but trampled
underfoot, vines and hops
swept aside by the flood

of battle, the apples blasted
from the trees, scattered
like grape-shot.

Gutted knapsacks, boots,
cavalry caps, jackets, swords,
mess-tins, bayonets,

canteens, firelocks, tunics,
sabres, epaulettes,
overturned baggage cars,

dead horses
with their legs in the air,
scattered everywhere,

dead bodies,
mostly of Turcos and Zouaves,
picked over by pickpockets,

one of them staggering
under a huge load of gold
watches and teeth.

Hands hanging in the trees
in lieu of fruit,
trunkless legs at their feet.

I will never forget one man
whose head rested
on a heap of apples,

his knees drawn up
to his chin, his eyes wide
open, seeming to inspect

the head of a Turco or Zouave
which, blown clean off,
lay like a cannonball in his lap.

What debris a ruined empire
leaves behind it!
By the time I reached Sedan

with my crippled horse,
it was almost impossible
to ride through the streets

without treading on
bayonets and sabres, heaps
of shakos, thousands

of imperial eagles
torn off infantry caps,
or knocking into stooks

of musketry and pikes.
I thought of Sevastopol,
mirrors in fragments

on the floors, beds
ripped open, feathers
in the rooms a foot deep,

chairs, sofas, bedsteads,
bookcases, picture-frames,
images of saints, shoes, boots,

bottles, physic jars,
the walls and doors
hacked with swords,

even the bomb-shelters
ransacked, though in one dug-out
I found a music-book

with a woman's name
in it, and a canary bird,
and a vase of wild flowers.

Notes

This book owes much to the work of the brilliant Anglo-Irish journalist William Howard Russell (1820-1907), who is generally regarded as the father of the art of war correspondence. His dispatches from the Crimea, published in *The Times*, and collected under the title *The War* (Routledge, London, 1855), were especially influential in shaping public attitudes to the management, and mismanagement, of war.

The poems 'The Indian Mutiny' and 'The War Correspondent' are especially indebted to his writing; in many instances I have taken his words *verbatim*, or have changed them only slightly to accommodate rhyme and rhythm.

A selection of his work, introduced by Max Hastings and edited by Roger Hudson, is published by The Folio Society (London, 1995).

'The War Correspondent' was first published in *The Times Literary Supplement*. Acknowledgement is also due to the editors of *The New Yorker, Poetry Ireland Review, Bloomsday*, and *Nua*.